Church Times Study Guide

Going by

G000075000

The Bible and Christian Ethics

Neil Messer

CANTERBURY
PRESS
Norwich

First published in 2006 by the Canterbury Press Norwich
(a publishing imprint of Hymns Ancient & Modern Limited,
a registered charity)
St Mary's Works, St Mary's Plain,
Norwich, Norfolk NR3 3BH

www.scm-canterburypress.co.uk

British Library Cataloguing in Publication data

A catalogue record for this book is available
from the British Library

ISBN 1-85311-766-8/978-1-85311-766-4

Typeset by Regent Typesetting, London
Printed and bound by
Gallpen Colour Print, Norwich

Contents

Introduction

Many readers of this booklet would probably agree that the Bible ought to have some influence on the way that Christians and churches live their lives, but might find it more difficult to say exactly *what* influence it should have. This booklet is intended to explore what influence the Bible should have on Christian living. If we ask how Christian people and communities *ought* to live their lives, we are entering the territory of Christian ethics, so the question that I have just posed could be re-phrased somewhat along the following lines: What role, or roles, should the Bible play in Christian ethics? In this booklet, we shall explore that question both in general terms and by looking at a specific moral issue. Before we do either of those things, though, it is worth thinking a little more about what might be meant by 'Christian ethics'.

Already, I have used the word 'ethics', and have also referred to a 'moral' issue. Over the years, much ink has been spilled by scholars trying to define 'ethics' and 'morality' precisely and to spell out the differences between the two. The detailed definitions and distinctions need not worry us too much at this stage: it will be enough to notice that when we use words like 'ethics' and 'morality', we are using language that has something to do with right and wrong, good and evil, obligation, value and so forth. If we are talking about ethics, we might be interested in what we ought (or ought not) to do, the way we ought to live our lives or the kind of people and communities we ought to be. If we use the phrase '*Christian* ethics', we are presumably locating our talk of right and wrong, obligation and value, etc., in some way in the context of Christian faith and life. Again, the scholarly literature contains lengthy discussions, which at the moment need not preoccupy us too much, about what the 'Christian' in 'Christian ethics' might signify (see MacNamara, 'The Distinctiveness of Christian Morality', for a helpful introduction to these discussions).

So what kinds of question will we find ourselves asking if we begin exploring Christian ethics? First, and most obviously, there will be questions about *what* we ought to do: the content of our decisions and our moral lives. What should I do in this situation? What (if anything) should I advise, encourage or tell others to do? What ought we, as a society, to permit or prohibit? The following exercise should give you some idea of the range of issues that could be included under the heading 'What to decide'.

Exercise

Look through one issue of a daily newspaper and identify all the stories you can that raise moral issues of this sort: issues about *what we or others ought to do*. Write down, as clearly and briefly as you can, what the questions are – for example, 'Should patients be entitled to have help from their doctors in committing suicide and, if so, under what circumstances?'

When you do this kind of exercise, you can discover a huge number of questions with 'ought' or 'should' in them, referring to every aspect of our private and public lives. There are questions about sex and relationships, the care, discipline and education of children and young people, how society should treat criminal offenders, medical care, particularly at the beginning and end of life, economics, international trade and development, the use of military power and much more besides. Questions of this sort are often labelled 'practical', 'applied' or 'substantive' ethics, though these terms have their problems.

However, these questions are not the only ones that Christian ethics is concerned with. When we are faced with moral decisions, particularly when the right choice is not obvious, a second sort of question arises: *How* should we decide? What criteria should we use to tell right from wrong? Where should we look for moral insight, guidance or authority? What influences should shape our moral judgements? Much of the time, of course, we do not bring these 'How?' questions out into the open – nor can we, if we are ever to *make* any decisions and get on with the business of living the lives that we are called to live. But whether we realize it or not, they are there in the background.

Suppose I discover that an old friend of mine is being sexually unfaithful to his partner and she does not know. Should I tell her? All kinds of arguments for and against might occur to me: she has a right to know the truth; he has a right to my loyalty; infidelity is wrong; it might cause them both pain if the truth comes out; it might cause *more* pain in the long run if it doesn't; I hate conflict and find emotional scenes embarrassing; he has been annoying me lately and this will be a good way to get back at him; and so on. Some of these reasons will weigh more heavily than others, and I will probably dismiss some of them as trivial, irrelevant or plain bad reasons for a decision about what I *ought* to do. The point is that, whether I am aware of it or not, my decision about what to do presupposes a whole set of decisions about *how to decide* what to do.

These decisions about how to decide may only be partly conscious, and will have been shaped by many factors: my upbringing, faith commitment, past experience and reflection, and so on. Also, in the future, I might look back on the decision I am making now and be critical of the way that I made it. Perhaps I should have paid more attention to the teaching of the Bible or the Church; perhaps I should have taken less notice of what I had been taught by my parents; perhaps I should have been more sensitive to the consequences of my actions. The next exercise invites you to reflect in this way on some of your own past moral experience.

Exercise

Write a brief description (one or two paragraphs) of a moral dilemma or situation from your personal experience. (It might, for example, be about a difficult decision that you or someone close to you has had to make.) Try to state as clearly as possible what the issue or dilemma was. Also state, as clearly as you can, how you (or the person in the situation) decided what to do: what were the reasons for and against; what factors influenced the decision; where did you, or they, look for guidance?

Keep your answer to this exercise – you will be invited to return to it towards the end of the booklet.

Questions of this second sort – the 'How?' questions – often go by descriptions such as 'moral theory', and 'ethical method'. One way to ask these questions in Christian ethics is to ask what its *sources* should be (in other words, where Christians should look for moral insight, guidance or authority), how those sources should be used and how they should be related to one another. One commonly used way to classify the sources is as *Scripture, tradition, reason* and *experience*.

By *Scripture*, Christians mean (roughly speaking) that diverse collection of writings that you will find between the covers of something labelled 'Holy Bible' in your local bookshop. Later on, we shall explore more fully what might be meant by calling this collection of writings 'Scripture', and what their significance for Christian ethics might be. *Tradition* often sounds to modern ears like something fusty and old-fashioned, but that is not what theologians mean to suggest when they use the word: biblical scholar Richard Hays defines it as 'the Church's time-honoured practices of worship, service and critical reflection' (Hays, *The Moral Vision of the New Testament*, p. 210). In some parts of the Church, tradition is closely linked to Church authority: the Church's leaders have the authority and responsibility for articulating the tradition and spelling out its implications for Christian faith and life. This is very roughly what is meant in Roman Catholicism by the 'Magisterium', or teaching authority, of the Church.

To describe *reason* as a source of Christian ethics is to say that by using our human powers of reasoning, we can work out at least some of what we need to know about the right and the good. Some secular theories of ethics have been, in effect, attempts to ground moral decision-making solely in human reason, avoiding appeals to received tradition, external authority or divine revelation. Some approaches to Christian ethics have also stressed reason as a source, setting great store by what 'any reasonable person' can discover of the right and the good. Other Christians have been much more suspicious of reason as a source, often on the grounds that human sinfulness distorts and limits our capacity to know what is truly good. The final category, *experience*, covers a variety of things. It can refer to the role of the individual's conscience in moral decision-making. It can point to an individual or corporate experience of the Holy Spirit's guidance. It can also refer to the approach often taken by feminist and liberation theologians, who argue that the starting point for theological and ethical reflection must be the experience of those who are oppressed and marginalized at the hands of the powerful.

The relationship between these sources can be set up in many different ways. For example, some Christians hold that Scripture is the *only* authority that Christians ought to recognize, and that tradition, reason and experience should be treated with some suspicion. Others recognize Scripture as the *ultimate* authority, but regard tradition, reason and experience as subordinate sources that have an indispensable role in helping us read and understand Scripture rightly. Still others hold that all the sources must be held in some kind of balance or creative tension, with none allowed to 'trump' the others.

As well as the 'What' and 'How' questions, there is a third kind of question that Christian ethics asks. We might call it, for short, the 'Who' question. The first two kinds of question are mostly about *acts* and *decisions* – *what* should I do, and *how do I know* what I should do? By contrast, the third kind of question asks 'What sort of people, and communities, ought we to *be*?' It is a question particularly associated with the approach known as 'virtue ethics', which has a very long history in western thought, and which has become very important and influential in recent Christian ethics. Some Christian ethicists would argue that the 'Who' questions are in fact the most basic and important ones. There is, of course, a two-way relationship between these questions and the others: if we have a virtuous *character* (if we are the right kind of people and community) we are more likely to make wise moral judgements and do the right thing; but our actions and decisions also help to *shape* our character, for good or for ill.

Some approaches to Christian ethics make something of a separation between ethical *theory* (the 'How' and 'Who' questions) and *practice* (the 'What' questions). This booklet takes a different approach. We shall explore a practical issue (the ethics of human cloning and stem cell research) together with a question of ethical theory (the use of the Bible in Christian ethics), asking what light each sheds on the other. What does the issue of cloning and stem cell research show us about the problems, challenges and opportunities of using the Bible in Christian ethics? And how do our conclusions about the Bible help us to address the challenges of cloning and stem cell research?

1

A Case Study: Human Cloning and Stem Cell Research

'Cloning' means producing a genetically identical copy of an already existing living organism. It is a natural means of reproduction for many plant and animal species (including, for example, some insects), but does not occur naturally in mammals. In the 1990s, Ian Wilmut and his team in Scotland made scientific history by developing a technique for cloning mammals artificially – most famously Dolly the sheep, who was first displayed to the public in 1997.

Wilmut's interest was in animal biotechnology, but speculation quickly turned to the possibility of cloning humans, and legislation and regulation soon followed. Human reproductive cloning (the use of the cloning technique to produce a live human being) is now against the law in Britain and many other countries. However, so-called 'therapeutic cloning' is permitted in Britain. This means using the cloning technique to produce embryos for use in medical research or the treatment of disease and injury. Many of these medical uses would take advantage of the fact that the cells of the early embryo are so-called 'totipotent stem cells' – that is, they have the capacity to develop into any of the specialized forms of cell found in the human body. Researchers believe that cloned stem cells could one day be used to replace dead or damaged cells in patients suffering from diseases such as Parkinson's, Alzheimer's or diabetes. Embryonic stem cells could be obtained from other sources, such as 'spare' embryos from IVF. However, the advantage of obtaining stem cells from embryos cloned from the patient him- or herself is that they would then be identical with the patient's own cells. This would make them less likely to be rejected by the patient's immune system.

It has not proved easy to produce cloned embryonic stem cells from humans, though many research groups around the world are working hard to do so. Early in 2004, a South Korean-led team claimed to have produced a cloned stem cell line, but just under two years later, their claim was retracted when the leader of the team admitted that some of the key data had been fabricated. However, other research groups, including one in the UK, have reported significant progress towards this goal.

Questions

- Can you think of any biblical commands, principles, stories or themes that might be relevant to this issue?
- What insights from tradition, reason and experience might also be relevant? How should these insights be related to any relevant insights from the Bible?
- Should Christians oppose or support human reproductive cloning, and why?
- Should Christians oppose or support human embryonic stem cell research for therapeutic purposes, and why?

If Christians wish to look to the Bible as a source of moral authority, they face various kinds of problem and challenge. On some issues, it looks fairly straightforward to appeal to the Bible's teaching on the subject. If we are wondering about the rightness or wrongness of remarriage after divorce, for example, there seems to be fairly clear teaching in the New Testament that prohibits it. Even in this kind of case, though, all is not what it seems. First, a careful reading reveals significant differences between the various New Testament texts that refer to divorce and remarriage. Secondly, some scholars argue that the social setting of first-century Palestine is so different from the twenty-first century West that these commands cannot be taken at face value by Christians in Western countries today.

There are more obvious problems in the case of cloning and stem cell research, since the Bible never mentions these things, nor the whole host of scientific, technological, political, social and cultural developments that modern Western readers take for granted but that could never even have been dreamt of by the Bible's authors. If the Bible is a source of authority for Christian ethics, does it have anything to say about such things, and how can we learn *what* it might have to say?

These problems require us to explore a little further what the Bible is and what might be involved in treating it as a source of authority for Christian ethics.

2

What Is the Bible and Why Is It Important?

If we call this particular collection of writings 'Scripture', we are setting it apart from other ancient texts. We are claiming that it is in some sense authoritative for the community of faith that calls it 'Scripture'. To put it like this makes it clear that 'Scripture' and 'Church' belong together. As ethicist Allen Verhey puts it (following theologian David Kelsey), they are 'correlative concepts' (Verhey, *Remembering Jesus*, p. 10). Each is defined with reference to the other: Scripture is the collection of writings that shapes the Church's identity; the Church is the community whose identity is shaped by these writings and the story they tell.

Why *these* writings and why not others? This is a question about the so-called *canon* of Scripture. 'Canon' comes from the Greek word for 'rule' or 'measuring rod', and in relation to the Bible, it means the list of books that are regarded as Scripture. It was, obviously, the Church that fixed the canon, deciding in the few centuries after Christ which writings were to be included. (Christians, of course, included in their canon an earlier collection: the books of the Law, the Prophets and the Writings, already regarded as Scripture by Jews, that Christians now refer to as the Old Testament or the Hebrew Bible.)

On one view, the fact that the Church fixed the canon means that the Church has some kind of authority over Scripture – it is the Church that determines which writings are to have this status. Another, more suspicious, view regards it as an exercise in power – that those who had influence in the early Church approved those texts that accorded with their understanding of the Christian faith and excluded dissenting voices. From this viewpoint, the canon of Scripture is history – and theology – written by the winning side. A third view, widely held by Protestant ethicists, regards the canon neither as the creation of the Church nor as imposed by those in power. Rather, the selection of the canonical writings was an act of discernment of those writings that truly *had* authority for

Christian faith and life. As Allen Verhey puts it, 'The Church did not so much create Scripture as acknowledge it as the texts within which the Spirit moved to give life and to guide' (Verhey, *Remembering Jesus*, p. 10).

It must also be remembered that Christians do not all agree on the extent of the canon. While the Catholic, Protestant and Orthodox Churches agree about most of the books to be included, each Church's selection is different in some respects to those of the other two. This is essentially because the Catholic and Orthodox Churches base their Old Testament canons on the Septuagint (the Greek translation of the Hebrew Scriptures widely used in the early Church), whereas, at the Reformation, the Protestants based their Old Testament canon on the Masoretic Text (the definitive collection of the Hebrew Scriptures that had been compiled within Judaism in the tenth century CE). The result is that there are books, and parts of books, recognized as Scripture by Catholics and Orthodox but not by most Protestants, and some texts only recognized by the Orthodox. These differences have sometimes contributed to theological controversies, though many scholars are inclined to play down the doctrinal significance of the differences.

What do we mean, though, by the 'authority' of Scripture? It is sometimes said that all Christian theologies (it might be truer to say most) treat Scripture as *somehow* authoritative. The question is, *how*? What is the nature of its authority? Some authors remain vague about this, but there is a range of clear positions taken by Christians and churches.

At one extreme is what is sometimes called a 'biblicist' view (it could also be called 'fundamentalist', but that word is so often used as a non-specific term of abuse that it seems best to avoid it in this discussion). Scripture is viewed as authoritative because it is divinely inspired – biblicists understand this to mean that the written words of the Bible (as originally written down, in the original manuscripts and languages) are the very words of God. The human authors wrote down the words that the Holy Spirit moved them to write, by a kind of divine dictation. Claims of infallibility follow from this, with some biblicists holding that nothing the Bible says can err in any respect and others saying, more modestly, that the Bible cannot err in relation to any matter of Christian faith or life.

In sharp contrast to the biblicist view is the notion that the Bible is the 'classic' of the Christian tradition. This view likens the Bible to those great works of literature, such as the plays of Shakespeare, that give profound and lasting insights into the human condition. It also suggests something about how the Bible should be used as a source of ethics. Thus, you might gain important moral insights from a play like *Othello*, but you would not think of using it as a rule book and you would search the text of the play in vain for ready-made answers to your questions about what you ought to do. If the Bible is a 'classic', it should no more be used in these ways than *Othello* should.

Furthermore, describing the Bible as the classic of the Christian tradition seems to suggest some kind of priority for *tradition* as a source of Christian faith. Christians down the ages have wrestled with questions about how they should live in response to the life, death and resurrection of Jesus Christ. The story of that wrestling and deliberation constitutes the moral tradition of the Church. The Bible is important not because its answers are definitive, but because it gives us a view of the earliest part of that tradition – the wrestling and deliberation of those who were closest in time to Jesus himself.

Somewhere between these two is a view that was well expressed by Allen Verhey some years ago (Verhey, 'Bible in Christian Ethics', p. 58). This view draws an analogy with Christology – the Christian doctrine of the person of Christ. In the person of Christ, there is a coming together of the human and the divine; some of the most important and complex theological debates in the early Church were attempts to find ways of speaking adequately about this union of the human with the divine. The boundaries were set by the Council of Chalcedon (451 CE), which insisted that the divine and human in the person of Christ must not be confused, divided, changed or separated. By analogy, in Scripture there is a coming together of the divine Word and the words of the human writers. In order to speak adequately about *this* union of the human with the divine, we must have an understanding of Scripture in which the divine Word and the human words are not confused, divided, changed or separated.

On this view, the problem with the biblicist understanding of Scripture is that it *confuses* the divine Word with the human words of the biblical writings, whereas some versions of the idea that the Bible is a 'classic' might risk *separating* the divine Word from the human words. By contrast, the great twentieth-century Protestant theologian Karl Barth understood the Bible in a way that lay firmly within Verhey's 'Chalcedonian' boundaries. Scripture, said Barth, is a unique witness to God's revelation of himself in Jesus Christ, and in it, we hear the Word of God thanks to the work of the Holy Spirit (Barth, *Church Dogmatics*, vol. I.2, pp. 457–537). It should be emphasized, though, that the 'Chalcedonian' view of Scripture is not restricted to Protestants: a number of Catholic thinkers, including the leading twentieth-century theologian Hans Urs von Balthasar, would hold similar views.

3

How Should the Bible be Used in Christian Ethics?

Some Christians – particularly those of a 'biblicist' mindset – tend to assume that the moral content of the Bible is a set of rules. Using the Bible in ethics means looking for the rule that will tell you what to do in your particular situation. If that is all there is to it, then some questions, such as remarriage after divorce, might seem to be settled fairly easily (though, as I said earlier, even here things might not be all that they seem). But Christian doctors and scientists wondering whether or not they should get involved in human stem cell research, and churches wondering whether to support or oppose it, will look in vain for guidance.

In fact, the moral content of the Bible is much richer and more varied than a set of rules could ever be. There are rules and commands, to be sure. Most famously, there are the Ten Commandments (Exodus 20.1–17, Deuteronomy 5.1–21), though even they are found in a 'narrative context' – that is, they come in the midst of the story of God's covenant with Israel. However, in Scripture, we find not only rules but also, as Richard Hays puts it, principles, paradigms and a symbolic world (Hays, *The Moral Vision of the New Testament*, pp. 208–9). By *principles*, he means general guidelines for conduct, such as the command to love God and your neighbour (Mark 12.28–31 and parallels, quoting Deuteronomy 6.4–5 and Leviticus 19.18). *Paradigms* are stories that give examples of conduct to either imitate or avoid. For example, Acts 4.36–7 tells the story of Barnabas' generosity to his fellow believers; 5.1–11 tells the cautionary tale of Ananias and Sapphira, who pretend to be generous like Barnabas, but are in fact trying to deceive the church, and come to a very bad end. Part of the message seems to be 'Be like Barnabas, not Ananias and Sapphira'. A *symbolic world* gives us the big picture of God, the world and ourselves. This big picture does not include any specific moral guidance, but does show us the general direction in which to find our moral bearings. For example, Matthew 5.43–8 shows us something of what God is like – indiscriminately generous to the good and the bad alike. Christian discipleship must respond to, and reflect, that generous love of God, but we have to work out for ourselves the details of what that might mean.

How, if at all, should this rich variety of ethical material guide Christians' moral lives, decisions and actions? Many writers on the Bible and ethics have been willing to look to the Bible for guidance at the levels of principle, paradigm and symbolic world, but have been extremely cautious about appealing directly to biblical rules. For example, in the 1970s, Leslie Houlden wrote that the New Testament 'yields certain perspectives, patterns and priorities, and it forms the Christian mind which then turns to the examination of contemporary issues – perhaps to apply central New Testament principles more rigorously than any of the New Testament writers' (Houlden, *Ethics and the New Testament*, pp. 119–20). One difficulty with appealing directly to biblical rules or commands is that the Bible does not speak with one voice. There are rules and commands that say very different things; some even seem to contradict one another. As I remarked earlier, even the apparently clear teaching of Jesus on divorce and remarriage comes in significantly different versions in different Gospels. Faced with the diversity of biblical material, those who take a 'biblicist' approach to scriptural rules and commands either have to select some and ignore others, or will find themselves doing intellectual gymnastics to try and show that apparently contradictory texts really mean the same thing.

The other major problem with appealing directly to biblical commands is that they come from places and times so different from ours. Attempting to read moral answers directly from the texts seems to ignore these great differences of context. For example, even if the New Testament prohibited divorce in the first century, it could be argued that changes in the status of women, the nature and purpose of marriage and the wider social context between the first century and the twenty-first mean that the prohibition simply does not apply any more. Perhaps, as Houlden argues, the same reasons that led New Testament authors to prohibit divorce in the first century should lead us in the opposite direction now (Houlden, *Ethics and the New Testament*, pp. 117–18).

Richard Hays takes a different view of biblical rules and commands. He argues that the presence in the canon of all four kinds of moral discourse – rules, principles, paradigms and symbolic worlds – suggests that all four are relevant to the Christian community. If we grant any text authority, it must be in the mode in which it speaks, so we should treat a rule *as* a rule rather than try to squeeze a principle out of it. However, although all four are needed, he believes that ethical material in *narrative* form should take precedence, because the New Testament is, above all, the *story* of God's work in Jesus Christ. (Hays, *Moral Vision*, pp. 294–5. His focus on narrative reflects a broader movement in recent theology, which has emphasized that some kinds of theological truth are best communicated in narrative form. Initially this may seem strange, since we sometimes tend to think that 'story' means 'fiction', whereas truth comes in the form of facts that can be stated in quasi-scientific propositions. Narrative theologians, however, argue that on the contrary, stories can be every bit as true as propositions; indeed, they can communicate kinds of truth that propositions are ill-adapted to convey.)

If we are to treat the ethical material of the Bible in this way, how are we to deal with the two problems I have highlighted – the diversity of the biblical texts and the differences between their context and ours? Hays sets out what he calls the 'fourfold task' of New Testament ethics, which, among other things, includes ways of dealing with these problems (Hays, *Moral Vision*, pp. 3–7). The first part is what he calls the *descriptive* task. This requires a careful reading of the texts that pays attention to all of them, not selecting out the ones we prefer, that is sensitive to the kinds of literature we are reading, and that takes note of what the texts *actually* say, not distorting them to make them say what we think they should. The next task he describes as *synthetic*. This means asking whether or not there is any overall message or coherent picture that emerges from all these diverse texts, without trying to squeeze them all into one mould.

The third stage is the *hermeneutical* task (the task of interpretation): this involves crossing the divide between the biblical writers' worlds and ours, asking what these ancient texts say to us in our modern world. Like other scholars, Hays stresses the crucial importance of the Christian community and its faith traditions in this task. As the community reads these texts carefully and prayerfully together, it can make creative and imaginative connections between the texts and the new situations that it faces. This is a risky enterprise, for which there are no set rules, but the Church has never been able to avoid it. Even the New Testament authors make these creative leaps of imagination by applying texts from the Hebrew Scriptures to new situations. A Christian community that does this humbly and prayerfully, says Hays, can trust in the Holy Spirit's guidance. The final task is closely linked to the third. Hays calls it the *pragmatic* task of acting on what we have learned and decided: no ethical deliberation is complete unless it results in action and affects the way we live.

Other scholars are more sceptical about many of the ways in which the Bible is used in Christian ethics. A good example is Tom Deidun ('The Bible and

Christian Ethics'), who points out the same problems that others, including Hays, recognize – the diversity of the biblical material, the time- and culture-bound nature of the writings, the fact that some of them were written to address very particular situations and needs, as well as the great gap between their worlds and ours. Deidun, however, makes more of these problems than Hays does, and takes ethicists to task for either ignoring them or taking them insufficiently seriously. He doubts that Hays' 'synthetic task' – finding a coherent overall message – is possible: he believes that those who look to the Bible for moral rules or principles tend to end up picking and choosing between texts in an arbitrary way.

Deidun himself is sympathetic to the so-called 'Autonomy' school of Roman Catholic ethics. According to this school of thought, Christian sources such as the Bible do not teach us anything new about the *content* of ethics, but might supply a specifically Christian *context* and *motivation* for our moral decision making. For example, one thing that the New Testament can do, according to Deidun, is remind us of the connections between Christian faith-experience and morality. Christians might come to the same moral conclusions as others; those conclusions, however, will be based not only on right reason, but also on their experience of God in Christ through the work of the Holy Spirit. Again, the New Testament gives a picture of the ways in which early Christian communities resolved their moral disputes and dilemmas; Deidun suggests that this picture might challenge the authority structures and decision-making processes of some present-day Christian Churches. (It is worth noting in passing that different views about the use of the Bible in Christian ethics do not divide neatly along the lines of different Christian traditions. Though Hays is a Protestant scholar and Deidun a Catholic, some Protestant thinkers would be sympathetic to Deidun's view, while some Catholics might well be closer to at least some aspects of Hays's position than to Deidun's.)

Hays and Deidun are both professional New Testament scholars, who would presumably agree on many technical questions about the study of the Bible, yet they come to radically different conclusions about its use in ethics. This is a reminder that Christians who agree about the problems and challenges of using the Bible may nevertheless disagree sharply about its status as a source of Christian ethics. These differences might not only be based on technical questions of biblical scholarship, but also be related in complex ways to much deeper theological and Church commitments.

Most of us will be instinctively drawn to one or other of the various positions in the debate about the Bible and ethics, but it is worth stepping back and taking a questioning look at our instincts. Someone like me, who tends to stress the authority of Scripture for Christian ethics, may need to be reminded by Deidun not to gloss over the difficulties. In contrast, someone who is inclined to stress the continuity between Christian ethics and the ethics of 'any reasonable person' may need to be reminded by Hays that the Church is sometimes called to be a countercultural community, witnessing to standards and ways of life that look decidedly *un*reasonable to the surrounding culture.

4

The Case Study Revisited: Human Cloning and Stem Cell Research

Earlier, I drew attention to the very obvious fact that the Bible has nothing directly to say about human cloning, stem cell research or a whole host of other ethical problems with which Christians are faced in the twenty-first century. Furthermore, it might seem that the Bible is so far removed from the intellectual, social and cultural context that makes human cloning and stem cell research possible that it cannot contribute anything relevant to these debates. However, Christians do in fact have plenty to say about cloning, stem cell research and other new problems, drawing in various ways on the Bible, as well as Christian tradition, reason and experience.

Most Christians who comment on human reproductive cloning agree that it would be wrong; this echoes a fairly widespread opposition to it in wider public and political debates. Much of the opposition in public debates, and to some extent in Christian arguments, stems from concerns about harmful consequences. As things stand with cloning technology at present, it is likely that a high proportion of human clones would either be stillborn or have serious congenital health problems. For some people, such arguments about consequences are all that need be said: they take what is known as a *consequentialist* approach to ethics, which evaluates actions solely in terms of their good and bad consequences. On this view, if human cloning could be made reasonably safe, and we could be satisfied that it would not result in other kinds of unacceptably harmful consequence (such as a diversion of healthcare resources away from more urgent needs), then it could be justified. However, many disagree. It is often said, both in Christian discussions and in wider debates, that, even if reproductive cloning could be made safe, it would still be wrong, because it would somehow threaten the worth and dignity of human beings.

This concern about human dignity is sometimes expressed rather vaguely, and writers who support reproductive cloning, such as John Harris, question this line of argument (Harris, *On Cloning*, pp. 34–66). There are Christian versions of it, however, that can be more precisely stated. Many Christian objections to reproductive cloning see it as a way of taking excessive control of human procreation and identity. In common with current reproductive technologies such as *in vitro* fertilization (IVF), it would introduce a large measure of technological control into procreation. In addition, it would allow us to determine fairly precisely the genetic make-up of the human beings produced by cloning. (It is worth stressing that this would not amount to anything like total control over the clones' personal identities. A human person's identity is the product of an almost unimaginably complex interaction between genetic inheritance, environmental factors that influence physical characteristics, a unique personal history of relationships, a social, cultural and political context, and so on. Even though cloning might allow us to control the genetic component of this mix, many of the other factors would almost certainly be impossible to control. This means that science fiction storylines about cloning great leaders, outstanding thinkers or tyrannical dictators are sheer fantasy. We might be able to replicate the *genotype* – the sum total of an individual's genes – but we could never replicate the *person*.)

Technological control of procreation and identity is seen as problematic in at least two ways. First, it marks a shift in our relationships with our fellow human beings. A number of years ago, Oliver O'Donovan borrowed the language of the Nicene Creed to draw a distinction between 'begetting' and 'making' (O'Donovan, *Begotten or Made?*). Those whom we *beget* are like us – they are fellow human beings who share our nature and command our respect. However, we do not have the same kind of relationship with things that we *make*: we can own and control them in ways that we cannot own or control our fellow humans. If we try to control human procreation technologically – particularly if we try to determine aspects of the identity of other humans – we are in danger of coming to regard them less as fellow humans who command our respect, and more as products or commodities that we can own and control. This would be bad, not only for those who were regarded as commodities, but for human society as a whole: it would be a radical distortion of the ways in which Christian faith teaches us to relate to one another.

Secondly, some Christians see this kind of technological control as an attempt (conscious or otherwise) to make ourselves like God the Creator, forgetting that we are not gods but God's creatures. Christians sometimes express this argument by referring to two texts from the book of Genesis: the second creation story, in which God commands the human being to cultivate the garden of Eden (Genesis 2.15) – in effect, a mandate to human beings to make something of the created world – and the story of the Tower of Babel (Genesis 11.1–9), in which humans use their technological skill to try and become like God, but fail and end up 'scattered . . . over the face of the earth'.

Many aspects of medicine and technology could, in principle, be like cultivating the garden of Eden – part of our human calling by God to make something of the world. However, it is argued, reproductive cloning would be more like building the Tower of Babel. In effect, we would be trying to make ourselves into creators of human beings, and would be in danger of deceiving ourselves that we can become like God by means of our own skill and cleverness. This would have the effect of alienating us from God: when we try to become like gods ourselves, we make ourselves unable to respond to God with the love, trust and worship that are the characteristics of a right relationship with God.

So-called 'therapeutic cloning' and stem cell research, however, would not necessarily be subject to these objections. There is a long tradition that sees medicine as a proper human and Christian calling, a way of following in the footsteps of Jesus the healer. Disease and suffering are contrary to God's loving purpose for human life – they are signs that things have gone badly wrong with the world. (This is not the only thing to say about them – they can also be opportunities for us to come to know God's love and goodness more fully – but this does not detract from the point that they are evils that can and should be resisted; see Barth, *Church Dogmatics*, vol. III.4, pp. 356–74.) When we use our knowledge and skill to resist the power of disease and suffering, we are doing the kind of work that God has given humans to do. When the purpose of stem cell research is directed at treating serious diseases, its aims and goals would seem to be in line with this Christian calling to heal. However, even though the *aims and goals* of stem cell research may be good, many Christians have concerns about the *means* used to pursue those goals. In particular, embryonic stem cells cannot be obtained without destroying human embryos. Therefore, we cannot decide on the morality of stem cell research without judging whether, and under what circumstances, it might be morally acceptable to destroy human embryos. To make that judgement, we shall need to think a little further about the human embryo itself.

The term 'embryo' refers to an individual during the first eight weeks of development after conception – from week nine onwards, it is referred to as a 'foetus'. In Britain, the law only allows experimentation (including stem cell research) on embryos up to 14 days old, which is the time after which the nervous system begins to form, and also the last point at which the embryo can split to form identical twins.

It is clear that the early embryo is, genetically, a human individual. Although its genetic material is derived from both parents, the embryo is genetically distinct from them and, except in the case of identical twins, unique. Furthermore, it has started out on a developmental path that, if nothing interrupts it, will result in the formation of an adult human. (It should be said that a high proportion of embryos fail to implant in the mother's womb and many pregnancies spontaneously terminate in their early stages, so, quite apart from any human intervention, many embryos do not become adult humans.) However, these facts by themselves do not tell us how human embryos should be treated.

To know how we should treat human embryos, we need some understanding of their *moral status*. What kind of entity is the embryo, and what moral responsibilities do we have concerning it? Broadly speaking, five answers to these two linked questions can be found in Christian (and other) writing on the embryo.

i The embryo is a person

Here, 'person' is a kind of philosophical shorthand for a being with the same kind of moral status that we accord to human children and adults. To say that the embryo is a person is to say, among other things, that it has the same kind of moral claims on us that human children and adults have. If there are ways in which we should never use children or adults (for example, deliberately killing them in order to harvest their organs for transplantation), then neither should we use embryos in equivalent ways (for example, destroying them in order to obtain stem cells for the medical treatment of others).

Christians who hold this view might argue that the embryo is in the early stages of a personal history that begins with conception, that the individual's life at every stage of that history is a gift from God, and that God loves and values the individual at every stage of her life, regardless of her characteristics, properties or abilities. There is no point after conception at which a line could be drawn that would mark the beginning of a new stage when the individual acquired a new kind of status or value in God's sight.

It is worth saying a little more at this stage about the concept of 'the person'. Its roots are in pre-Christian Greece and Rome, but it was first developed into a philosophically and theologically significant term by the thinkers of the early Church, who needed to find a language for speaking about the triune God and the person of Jesus Christ. However, the concept has gone through many twists and turns in Western thought, and some philosophers now use it in ways that are very different from the ways in which earlier thinkers would have spoken of either a divine or human person. Some of these characteristically modern ways of thinking about the person lie behind the next two positions on the status of the embryo.

ii The embryo is no more than a piece of human tissue

Those who hold this view might argue that the early embryo (certainly in the first two weeks after conception) has none of the abilities or properties that normally lead us to recognize human children and adults as persons. For example, it is not aware of itself, cannot suffer, cannot have relationships with others and cannot have interests, desires or plans. It should be regarded, morally speaking, in much the same way as we would a human organ or sample of tissue. We should be free to use it for the benefit of others in ways that we would not be free to use a human child or adult. For example, if we are free to use a human blood sample as a source of cells for medical research or treatment, we should be free to use a human embryo in the same way.

iii The embryo is a potential person, with a status somewhere between that of human tissue and that of a person

Those who hold this view might agree that the embryo cannot be counted as a person because it lacks the properties and abilities that normally lead us to recognize an individual as a person. Nonetheless, they might argue, it has the *potential* to develop into a person, and this potential entitles it to a special moral status – not as high as that of a person, but higher than that of a piece of human tissue. This might mean that it is morally justified to use embryos in medical research and treatment, but only if the benefits of the research or treatment are great and cannot be obtained in other ways. Something like this view was expressed by the majority report of the Warnock Committee, on which British legislation on reproductive technology and embryo research is based (*The Warnock Report*, pp. 58–69).

iv We do not know the status of the embryo

Those who take this view might simply mean that the status of the embryo is a complex issue about which we have not yet found a position that we can all agree on. However, they might mean, more fundamentally, that it is an issue that *cannot* be decided in a way that would help us rule on how embryos should be treated, because there is no consensus on the meaning of the basic concepts and assumptions that we would have to use in order to decide whether or not the embryo is a person. Sometimes, this view – that we do not, and perhaps cannot, know the status of the embryo for certain – is used to support conclusions similar to position (iii) – the embryo is entitled to some protection, but not as much as a human child or adult. However, Robert Song and others have argued that if we do not know the embryo's status, then we should err on the side of caution and treat it as a person. If we do not, we are opening ourselves to the possibility of committing a grave moral wrong. As Song puts it, quoting Germain Grisez, 'To be willing to kill what for all one knows is a person is to be willing to kill a person' (Song, 'To Be Willing to Kill').

v The question 'Is the embryo a person?' is the wrong question to ask

This argument can be found in a number of Christian discussions. For example, Richard Hays argues in this way about the moral status of the foetus in relation to abortion, and his argument can easily be extended to the embryo (Hays, *Moral Vision*, p. 451). He draws an analogy with the exchange between Jesus and the lawyer in Luke 10.25–37. Referring to the command to love your neighbour as yourself, the lawyer asks, 'And who is my neighbour?' Luke comments that he '[wants] to justify himself', to place limits on the range of people to whom he is obliged to show care and concern. Instead of answering him directly, Jesus replies with the parable of the Good Samaritan, which unsettles any attempt to draw a line between those who are, and those who are not, our neighbours. In the same way, Hays suggests, the question 'Who is a person?' functions as a self-interested way of setting limits to our moral concern. The parable of the Good

Samaritan should unsettle those limits and force us to find different ways of thinking about our moral obligations regarding embryos and foetuses.

Questions

- Of the five possible answers outlined above to the question about the status of the human embryo, which do you find most satisfactory and why? What does your preferred answer suggest about the morality of embryonic stem cell research?
- Return to your earlier conclusions about human reproductive cloning. In the light of the discussion in this section, how, if at all, would you now add to, or change, those conclusions?

Conclusion

It should be clear from the discussion in the last section that even when Christians are faced with new issues, such as human cloning and stem cell research, that could not have been imagined by the biblical writers, they still find many ways in which to use the Bible as a source for their moral deliberation. Using Hays's terminology, there may not be any biblical *rules* that apply directly, but Christians do appeal to *principles*, such as the command to love our neighbours, *paradigms* (as in Hays's use of the Good Samaritan story), and the *symbolic world* evoked by passages such as the Genesis 2 creation narrative and the story of the Tower of Babel. These biblical images and insights interact with themes from the Christian *tradition*, such as the complex history of the concept of 'person', the insights of *reason*, including relevant scientific information, and *experience*, including the experience of patients who might benefit from the treatments offered by stem cell research. The final exercise is an invitation to summarize and review the view you have formed of the role that the Bible should play in Christian ethics, and the way in which it should interact with tradition, reason and experience.

Exercise

Return to your response to the second exercise in the Introduction. Having worked through this booklet, would there now be anything different about the way in which you would make moral decisions of the kind you described in that response?

References

Karl Barth, *Church Dogmatics*, English trans. ed. by G. W. Bromiley and T. F. Torrance, Edinburgh: T & T Clark, 1956–77.

Tom Deidun, 'The Bible and Christian Ethics', in Bernard Hoose (ed.), *Christian Ethics: An Introduction*, London: Cassell, 1998, pp. 3–46.

John Harris, *On Cloning*, London and New York: Routledge, 2004.

Richard B. Hays, *The Moral Vision of the New Testament*, Edinburgh: T & T Clark, 1997.

Leslie Houlden, *Ethics and the New Testament*, London and Oxford: Mowbray, 1975.

Vincent MacNamara, 'The Distinctiveness of Christian Morality', in Hoose, *Christian Ethics*, pp. 149–60.

Oliver O'Donovan, *Begotten or Made?*, Oxford: Oxford University Press, 1984.

Robert Song, 'To Be Willing to Kill What for All One Knows Is a Person Is to Be Willing to Kill a Person', in Brent Waters and Ronald Cole-Turner (eds), *God and the Embryo: Religious Voices on Stem Cells and Cloning*, Washington, DC: Georgetown University Press, 2003, pp. 98–107.

Allen Verhey, 'Bible in Christian Ethics', in John Macquarrie and James Childress (eds), *A New Dictionary of Christian Ethics*, London: SCM Press, 1986, pp. 57–61.

Allen Verhey, *Remembering Jesus: Christian Community, Scripture, and the Moral Life*, Grand Rapids, MI: Eerdmans, 2002.

Mary Warnock (Chairman), *Report of the Committee of Inquiry into Human Fertilisation and Embryology (The Warnock Report)*, London: Her Majesty's Stationery Office, 1984.

Suggestions for Further Reading

The Bible and Christian Ethics

There is a big body of literature on this topic, the works listed below forming only a small selection from it. The discussion in this booklet has focused on the New Testament, saying little about the use of the Hebrew Bible in Christian ethics. It has also said little about the ethics of Jesus and has not dealt directly with the distinctive ways of using Scripture in feminist and liberation theologies. The following works should help to fill some of these gaps.

John Barton, *Ethics and the Old Testament*, London: SCM Press, 1998.

Robin Gill (ed.), *The Cambridge Companion to Christian Ethics*, Cambridge: Cambridge University Press, 2001. Chapters 2–5 discuss the Bible and Christian ethics; chapter 9 is on liberation theology.

Colin Hart, *The Ethics of Jesus*, Grove Ethical Studies no. 107, Cambridge: Grove, 1997.

Richard B. Hays, *The Moral Vision of the New Testament*, Edinburgh: T & T Clark, 1997.

Daniel L. Migliore, *Faith Seeking Understanding: An Introduction to Christian Theology*, Grand Rapids, MI: Eerdmans, 1991, chapters 2 and 3.

The New Testament Gateway at: www.ntgateway.com (accessed 9 September 2005). A valuable collection of online resources on the New Testament, including material on the canon and the historical Jesus.

Human Cloning and Embryonic Stem Cell Research

Ronald Cole-Turner (ed.), *Human Cloning: Religious Responses*, Louisville, KY: Westminster John Knox, 1997.

John Habgood, *Being a Person: Where Faith and Science Meet*, London: Hodder and Stoughton, 1998.

David Albert Jones, *The Soul of the Embryo: An Enquiry into the Status of the Human Embryo in the Christian Tradition*, London: Continuum, 2004.

Neil Messer, *The Ethics of Human Cloning*, Grove Ethical Studies no. 122, Cambridge: Grove, 2001.

Brent Waters, *Reproductive Technology: Towards a Theology of Procreative Stewardship*, London: Darton, Longman & Todd, 2001.

Brent Waters and Ronald Cole-Turner (eds), *God and the Embryo: Religious Voices on Stem Cells and Cloning*, Washington, DC: Georgetown University Press, 2003.